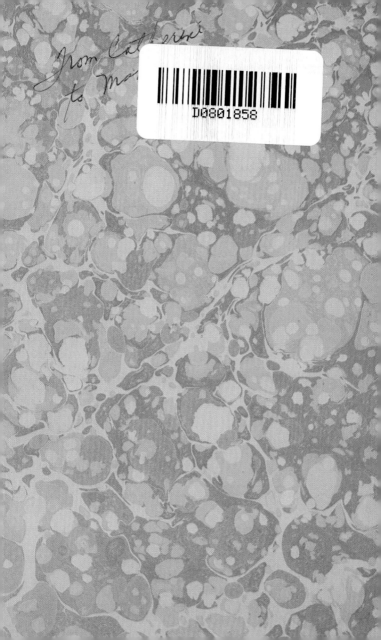

D0801858

THE ILLUSTRATED POETS

THE ILLUSTRATED POETS
Thomas Hardy

Selected and with an introduction
by Geoffrey Moore

AURUM PRESS

First published 1990 by Aurum Press Ltd,
10 Museum Street, London WC1A 1JS
Selection and introduction copyright © 1990 by Geoffrey Moore

British Library Cataloguing in Publication Data

Hardy, Thomas, *1840–1928*
Thomas Hardy – (The illustrated poets).
I. Title   II. Moore, Geoffrey, *1920–*   III. Series 821′.8

ISBN 1 85410 106 4

3   5   7   9   10   8   6   4   2
1991   1993   1995   1994   1992

Picture research by Juliet Brightmore

Printed in Hong Kong by Imago

CONTENTS

Introduction	10
Hap	13
She, to Him II	14
Neutral Tones	16
Friends Beyond	17
I Look Into My Glass	21
I Need Not Go	22
At Casterbridge Fair II, Former Beauties	25
Wessex Heights	26
The Going	30
I Found Her Out There	33
The Darkling Thrush	36
Great Things	38
The Roman Road	41
In Time of 'The Breaking of Nations'	42
The Voice	44
The Oxen	45
Weathers	46
Channel Firing	48
Bags of Meat	50
Snow in the Suburbs	53
Suspense	54
Afterwards	56
Squire Hooper	58
Notes	61

INTRODUCTION

Thomas Hardy was born in 1840 in the village of Upper Bockhampton, near Dorchester in Dorset, where his father worked as a master-mason. After four years' apprenticeship, he went at the age of twenty-two to London, where he worked for the well-known architect, Arthur Blomfield. But if architecture was his vocation, it was not his avocation. He wanted, above all, to be a poet. However, after trying for five years, he failed to find a publisher. Saddened, he returned to Dorchester, where he turned his hand, almost casually, to writing the novels for which he is so justly famous. When, in 1896, *Jude the Obscure* was received with hostility, however, he turned back to his first love, the writing of poetry.

This time the situation was very different. As an established novelist his verse was received with respect. Hardy's first book of poetry, *Wessex Poems*, came out in 1898. He was then fifty-eight and had published fourteen novels and more than forty short stories. There were seven more books of verse to come, the second, *Poems of the Past and the Present*, appearing in 1901, the year of Queen Victoria's death. Since his last book, *Winter Words*, was published in 1928, Hardy spans the Edwardian, neo-Georgian and the Victorian eras.

He expressed his hesitation at continuing to publish the work of a mid-Victorian in the seven-page 'Apology' which he wrote as a preface to *Late Lyrics and Earlier* in 1922. However, the main burden of his remarks concerns objections to 'the dark gravity' of his ideas. For such a label to be applied to a poet of Hardy's range and

seriousness betokens a very odd view of life and literature – as if an artist had the God-ordained task of illustrating 'the brighter side of life'. As he himself says, his so-called 'pessimism' arises from the need he feels to explore reality 'and is the first step towards the soul's betterment, and the body's also'.

The difficulty, for some, with Hardy's verse has nothing to do with his so-called 'view of life'. It has to do with his technique. As R. P. Blackmur, one of the most percipient of twentieth-century commentators on poetry, says in *Language as Gesture*, 'Hardy is the great example of a sensibility violated by ideas; and perhaps the unique example, since Swift, of a sensibility great enough – locked enough in life – to survive the violation.'

This is where Hardy's poetry is so deceptive, for he was interested in more than the mere conveying of ideas. Although he seems on the surface to be the poet of the Common Man – direct, blunt, having something to say and saying it – he is at his best a poet of great depth and subtlety. He had absorbed the Elizabethan and Jacobean poets and steeped himself in the work of Blake and Shelley – whose example he probably followed when he wrote his long dramatic verse poem, *The Dynasts*, about the Napoleonic War.

Hardy's greatness, however, lies in his short lyrics, which are written in so many styles that it is difficult to say – as one can of Hopkins or Yeats – that they could not have been written by anyone else. But, this stated, the pertinacity and strength of character which produced such an impressive body of work cannot but be admired. Who but Hardy could have realized the Dorset echoes of 'Friends Beyond' or, later in life, 'Squire Hooper'? The 1914 poem 'Channel Firing' is a salutary counterblast to Rupert Brooke's rhetoric. The shocking 'Bags of Meat' predates contemporary feeling about animals. Above all, Hardy's love poems show the soul of the man. Those written to his first wife, Emma, after her death in 1912 ('The Going', 'I Found Her Out There' and 'The Voice') are particularly moving.

At the heart of Hardy's work is Wessex (his name for Dorset). If he steeped himself in the Romantics, he also admired the verse of William Barnes, who wrote in Dorset dialect. Except for three periods away from the area, Hardy lived all his life in the county of his birth, returning there permanently for the last forty-five years of his life. He felt, rightly, that 'a certain provincialism of feeling is invaluable', for it is by being rooted in the local and particular that a writer may achieve universality.

W. H. Auden, who was influenced at an early age by Hardy's poetry, says, 'He was a good poet, perhaps a great one, but not *too* good.' He was essentially human. In *The Catcher in the Rye* J. D. Salinger gives us Holden Caulfield's test for a great writer – he is the one who, when you read him, you feel like ringing up. Thomas Hardy is just such a writer. However gloomy his view of life, he did not despise it. The heart of his philosophy is not nihilism but love. He was his own man; he went his own way. If we have the patience to follow him, we may find in his work rewards which we cannot easily find elsewhere.

GEOFFREY MOORE

Hap

If but some vengeful god would call to me
From up the sky, and laugh: 'Thou suffering thing,
Know that thy sorrow is my ecstasy,
That thy love's loss is my hate's profiting!

Then would I bear it, clench myself, and die,
Steeled by the sense of ire unmerited;
Half-eased in that a Powerfuller than I
Had willed and meted me the tears I shed.

But not so. How arrives it joy lies slain,
And why unblooms the best hope ever sown?
– Crass Casualty obstructs the sun and rain,
And dicing Time for gladness casts a moan . . .
These purblind Doomsters had as readily strown
Blisses about my pilgrimage as pain.

She, to Him II

Perhaps, long hence, when I have passed away,
Some other's feature, accent, thought like mine,
Will carry you back to what I used to say,
And bring some memory of your love's decline.

Then you may pause awhile and think, 'Poor jade!'
And yield a sign to me – as ample due,
Not as the tittle of a debt unpaid
To one who could resign her all to you –

And thus reflecting, you will never see
That your thin thought, in two small words
        conveyed
Was no such fleeting phantom-thought to me,
But the Whole Life wherein my part was played;
And you amid its fitful masquerade
A Thought – as I in your life seem to be!

Neutral Tones

We stood by a pond that winter day,
And the sun was white, as though chidden of God,
And a few leaves lay on the starving sod;
      – They had fallen from an ash, and were gray.

Your eyes on me were as eyes that rove
Over tedious riddles of years ago;
And some words played between us to and fro
      On which lost the more by our love.

The smile on your mouth was the deadest thing
Alive enough to have strength to die;
And a grin of bitterness swept thereby
      Like an ominous bird a-wing . . .

Since then, keen lessons that love deceives,
And wrings with wrong, have shaped to me
Your face, and the God-curst sun, and a tree,
      And a pond edged with grayish leaves.

Friends Beyond

William Dewy, Tranter Reuben, Farmer Ledlow
　　　late at plough,
　　　　　Robert's, kin, and John's, and Ned's,
And the Squire, and Lady Susan, lie in Melstock
　　　churchyard now!

'Gone,' I call them, gone for good, that group of
　　　local hearts and heads;
　　　　　Yet at mothy curfew-tide,
And at midnight then the noon-heat breathes it
　　　back from walls and leads,

They've a way of whispering to me – fellow-wight
　　　who yet abide –
　　　　　In the muted, measured note
Of a ripple under archways, or a lone cave's
　　　stillicide:

'We have triumphed: this achievement turns the
　　　bane to antidote,
　　　　　Unsuccesses to success,
Many thought-worn eves and morrows to a morrow
　　　free of thought.

'No more need we corn and clothing, feel of old
    terrestrial stress;
        Chill detraction stirs no sigh;
Fear of death has even bygone us: death gave all
    that we possess.'

W.D. – 'Ye mid burn the old bass-viol that I set
    such value by.'
Squire. – 'You may hold the manse in fee,
        You may wed my spouse, may let my children's
        memory of me die.'
Lady S. – 'You may have my rich brocades, my
    laces; take each household key;
        Ransack coffer, desk, bureau;
    Quiz the few poor treasures hid there, con the
        letters kept by me.'

Far. – 'Ye mid zell my favourite heifer, ye mid let
    the charlock grow,
        Foul the grinterns, give up thrift.'
Far. Wife. – 'If ye break my best blue china,
    children, I shan't care or ho.'

All. – 'We've no wish to hear the tidings; how the
     people's fortunes shift;
          What your daily doings are;
     Who are wedded, born, divided; if your lives
          beat slow or swift.

'Curious not the least are we if our intents you
     make or mar,
          If you quire to our old tune,
If the City stage still passes, if the weirs still roar
     afar.'

– Thus, with very gods' composure, freed those
     crosses late and soon
          Which, in life, the Trine allow
(Why, non witteth), and ignoring all that haps
     beneath the moon,

William Dewy, Tranter Reuben, Farmer Ledlow
     late at plough,
          Robert's kin, and John's, and Ned's,
And the Squire, and Lady Susan, murmur mildly to
     me now.

I Look Into My Glass

I look into my glass,
And view my wasting skin,
And say, 'Would God it came to pass
My heart had shrunk as thin!'

For then, I, undistrest
By hearts grown cold to me,
Could lonely wait my endless rest
With equanimity.

But Time, to make me grieve,
Part steals, lets part abide;
And shakes this fragile frame at eve
With throbbings of noontide.

I Need Not Go

I need not go
Through sleet and snow
To where I know
She waits for me;
She will tarry me there
Till I find it fair,
And have time to spare
From company.

When I've overgot
The world somewhat,
When things cost not
Such stress and strain,
Is soon enough
By cypress sough
To tell my Love
I am come again.

And if some day,
When none cries nay,
I still delay
To seek her side,
(Though ample measure
Of fitting leisure
Await my pleasure)
She will not chide.

What – not upbraid me
That I delayed me,
Nor ask what stayed me
So long? Ah, no! –
New cares may claim me,
New loves inflame me,
She will not blame me,
But suffer it so.

At Casterbridge Fair II
Former Beauties

These market-dames, mid-aged, with lips thin-
    drawn,
      And tissues sere,
Are the ones we loved in years agone,
      And courted here?

Are these the muslined pink young things to whom
      We vowed and swore
In nooks on summer Sundays by the Froom,
      Or Budmouth shore?

Do they remember those gay tunes we trod
      Clasped on the green;
Aye; trod till moonlight set on the beaten sod
      A satin sheen?

The must forget, forget! They cannot know
      What once they were,
Or memory would transfigure them, and show
      Them always fair.

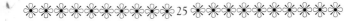

Wessex Heights

There are some heights in Wessex, shaped as if by a
    kindly hand
For thinking, dreaming, dying on, and at crises
    when I stand,
Say, on Ingpen Beacon eastward, or on Wylls-
    Neck westwardly,
I seem where I was before my birth, and after death
    may be.

In the lowlands I have no comrade, not even the
    lone man's friend –
Her who suffereth long and is kind; accepts what he
    is too weak to mend:
Down there they are dubious and askance; there
    nobody thinks as I,
But mind-chains do not clank where one's next
    neighbour is the sky.

In the towns I am tracked by phantoms having
    weird detective ways –
Shadows of beings who fellowed with myself of
    earlier days:
They hang about at places, and they say harsh
    heavy things –
Men with a wintry sneer, and women with tart
    disparagings.

Down there I seem to be false to myself, my simple
    self that was,
And is not now, and I see him watching,
    wondering what crass cause
Can I have merged him into such a strange
    continuator as this,
Who yet has something in common with himself,
    my chrysalis.

I cannot go to the great grey Plain; there's a figure
    against the moon,
Nobody sees it but I, and it makes my breast beat
    out of tune;
I cannot go to the tall-spired town, being barred by
    the forms now passed
For everybody but me, in whose long vision they
    stand there fast.

There's a ghost at Yell'ham Bottom chiding loud at
    the fall of the night,
There's a ghost in Froom-side Vale, thin-lipped
    and vague, in a shroud of white,
There is one in the railway train whenever I do not
    want it near,
I see its profile against the pane, saying what I
    would not hear.

As for one rare fair woman, I am now but a thought
    of hers,
I enter her mind and another thought succeeds me
    that she prefers;
Yet my love for her in its fulness she herself even
    did not know;
Well, time cures hearts of tenderness, and now I
    can let her go.

So I am found on Ingpen Beacon, or on Wylls-
    Neck to the west,
Or else on homely Bulbarrow, or little Pilsdon
    Crest,
Where men have never cared to haunt, nor women
    have walked with me,
And ghosts then keep their distance; and I know
    some liberty.

The Going

Why did you give no hint that night
That quickly after the morrow's dawn,
And calmly, as if indifferent quite,
You would close your term here, up and be gone
  Where I could not follow
  With wing of swallow
To gain one glimpse of you ever anon!

  Never to bid good-bye,
    Or lip me the softest call,
Or utter a wish for a word, while I
Saw morning harden upon the wall,
  Unmoved, unknowing
    That your great going
Had place that moment, and altered all.

Why do you make me leave the house
And think for a breath it is you I see
At the end of the alley of bending boughs
Where so often at dusk you used to be;
  Till in darkening dankness
  The yawning blankness
Of the perspective sickens me!

You were she who abode
       By those red-veined rocks far West,
You were the swan-necked one who rode
Along the beetling Beeny Crest,
       And, reining nigh me,
       Would muse and eye me,
While Life unrolled us its very best.

Why, then, latterly did we not speak,
Did we not think of those days long dead,
And ere your vanishing strive to seek
That time's renewal? We might have said,
       'In this bright spring weather
       We'll visit together
Those places that once we visited.'

       Well, well! All's past amend,
       Unchangeable. It must go.
I seem but a dead man held on end
To sink down soon . . . O you could not know
       That such swift fleeing
       No soul foreseeing –
Not even I – would undo me so!

I Found Her Out There

I found her out there
On a slope few see,
That falls westwardly
To the salt-edged air,
Where the ocean breaks
On the purple strand,
And the hurricane shakes
The solid land.

I brought her here,
And have laid her to rest
In a noiseless nest
No sea beats near.
She will never be stirred
In her loamy cell
By the waves long heard
And loved so well.

So she does not sleep
By those haunted heights
The Atlantic smites
And the blind gales sweep,
Whence she often would gaze
At Dundagel's famed head,
While the dipping blaze
Dyed her face fire-red;

And would sigh at the tale
Of sunk Lyonnesse,
As a wind-tugged tress
Flapped her cheek like a flail;
Or listen at whiles
With a thought-bound brow
To the murmuring miles
She is far from now.

Yet her shade, maybe,
Will creep underground
Till it catch the sound
Of that western sea
As it swells and sobs
Where she once domiciled,
And joy in its throbs
With the heart of a child.

The Darkling Thrush

I leant upon a coppice gate
    When Frost was spectre-gray,
And Winter's dregs made desolate
    The weakening eye of day.
The tangled bine-stems scored the sky
    Like strings of broken lyres,
And all mankind that haunted nigh
    Had sought their household fires.

The land's sharp features seemed to be
    The Century's corpse outleant,
His crypt the cloudy canopy,
    The wind his death-lament.
The ancient pulse of germ and birth
    Was shrunken hard and dry,
And every spirit upon earth
    Seemed fervourless as I.

At once a voice arose among
      The bleak twigs overhead
In a full-hearted evensong
      Of joy illimited;
An aged thrush, frail, gaunt, and small,
      In blast-beruffled plume,
Had chosen thus to fling his soul
      Upon the growing gloom.

So little cause for carolings
      Of such ecstatic sound
Was written on terrestrial things
      Afar or nigh around,
That I could think there trembled through
      His happy good-night air
Some blessed Hope whereof he knew
      And I was unaware.

Great Things

Sweet cyder is a great thing,
　　A great thing to me,
Spinning down to Weymouth town
　　By Ridgway thirstily,
And maid and mistress summoning
　　Who tend the hostelry:
O cyder is a great thing,
　　A great thing to me!

The dance it is a great thing,
　　A great thing to me,
With candles lit and partners fit
　　For night-long revelry;
And going home when day-dawning
　　Peeps pale upon the lea:
O dancing is a great thing,
　　A great thing to me!

Love is, yea, a great thing,
    A great thing to me,
When, having drawn across the lawn
    In darkness silently,
A figure flits like one a-wing
    Out from the nearest tree:
O love is, yes, a great thing,
    A great thing to me!

Will these be always great things,
    Great things to me? . . .
Let it befall that One will call,
    'Soul, I have need of thee:'
What then? Joy-jaunts, impassioned flings,
    Love, and its ecstasy,
Will always have been great things,
    Great things to me!

The Roman Road

The Roman Road runs straight and bare
As the pale parting-line in hair
Across the heath. And thoughtful men
Contrast its days of Now and Then,
And delve, and measure, and compare;
Visioning on the vacant air
Helmed legionaries, who proudly rear
The Eagle, as they pace again
                The Roman Road.

But no tall brass-helmed legionnaire
Haunts it for me. Uprises there
A mother's form upon my ken,
Guiding my infant steps, as when
We walked that ancient thoroughfare,
                The Roman Road.

In Time of 'The Breaking of Nations'

I

Only a man harrowing clods
    In a slow silent walk
With an old horse that stumbles and nods
    Half asleep as they stalk.

II

Only thin smoke without flame
    From the heaps of couch-grass;
Yet this will go onward the same
    Though Dynasties pass.

III

Yonder a maid and her wight
    Come whispering by:
War's annals will cloud into night
    Ere their story die.

The Voice

Woman much missed, how you call to me, call to
    me,
Saying that now you are not as you were
When you had changed from the one who was all
    to me,
But as at first, when our day was fair.

Can it be you that I hear? Let me view you, then,
Standing as when I drew near to the town
Where you would wait for me: yes, as I knew you
    then,
Even to the original air-blue gown!

Or is it only the breeze, in its listlessness
Travelling across the wet mead to me here,
You being ever dissolved to wan wistlessness,
Heard no more again far or near?

    Thus I; faltering forward,
    Leaves around me falling,
Wind oozing thin through the thorn from norward,
    And the woman calling.

The Oxen

Christmas Eve, and twelve of the clock.
    'Now they are all on their knees,'
An elder said as we sat in a flock
    By the embers in hearthside ease.

We pictured the meek mild creatures where
    They dwelt in their strawy pen,
Nor did it occur to one of us there
    To doubt they were kneeling then.

So fair a fancy few would weave
    In these years! Yet, I feel,
If someone said on Christmas Eve,
    'Come; see the oxen kneel

'In the lonely barton by yonder coomb
    Our childhood used to know,'
I should go with him in the gloom,
    Hoping it might be so.

Weathers

I

This is the weather the cuckoo likes,
    And so do I;
When showers betumble the chestnut spikes,
    And nestlings fly:
And the little brown nightingale bills his best,
And they sit outside at 'The Travellers' Rest',
And maids come forth sprig-muslin drest,
And citizens dream of the south and west,
    And so do I.

II

This is the weather the shepherd shuns,
    And so do I;
When beeches drip in browns and duns,
    And thresh, and ply;
And hill-hid tides throb, throe on throe,
And meadow rivulets overflow,
And drops on gate-bars hang in a row,
And rooks in families homeward go,
    And so do I.

Channel Firing

That night your great guns, unawares,
Shook all our coffins as we lay,
And broke the chancel window-squares,
We thought it was the Judgement-day

And sat upright. While drearisome
Arose the howl of wakened hounds:
The mouse let fall the altar-crumb,
The worms drew back into the mounds,

The glebe cow drooled. Till God called, 'No;
It's gunnery practice out at sea
Just as before you went below;
The world is as it used to be:

'All nations striving strong to make
Red war yet redder. Mad as hatters
They do no more for Christés sake
Than you who are helpless in such matters.

'That this is not the judgement-hour
For some of them's a blessed thing,
For if it were they'd have to scour
Hell's floor for so much threatening . . .

'Ha, ha. It will be warmer when
I blow the trumpet (if indeed
I ever do; for you are men,
And rest eternal sorely need).'

So down we lay again. 'I wonder,
Will the world ever saner be,'
Said one, 'than when He sent us under
In our indifferent century!'

And many a skeleton shook his head.
'Instead of preaching forty year,'
My neighbour Parson Thirdly said,
'I wish I had stuck to pipes and beer.'

Again the guns disturbed the hour,
Roaring their readiness to avenge,
As far inland as Stourton Tower,
And Camelot, and starlit Stonehenge.

Bags of Meat

Here's a fine bag of meat,'
Says the master-auctioneer,
As the timid, quivering steer,
Starting a couple of feet
At the prod of a drover's stick,
And trotting lightly and quick,
A ticket stuck on his rump,
Enters with a bewildered jump.

'Where he's lived lately, friends,
I'd live till lifetime ends:
They've a whole life everyday
Down there in the Vale, have they!
He'd be worth the money to kill
And give away Christmas for good-will.'

'Now here's a heifer – worth more
Than bid, were she bone-poor;
Yet she's round as a barrel of beer;'
'She's a plum,' said the second auctioneer.

'Now this young bull – for thirty pound?
Worth that to manure your ground!'
'Or to stand,' chimed the second one,
'And have his picter done!'
The beast was rapped on the horns and snout
To make him turn about.
'Well,' cried a buyer, 'another crown –
Since I've dragged here from Taunton Town!'

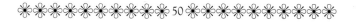

'That calf, she sucked three cows,
Which is not matched for bouse
In the nurseries of high life
By the first-born of a nobleman's wife!'
The stick falls, meaning, 'A true tale's told,'
On the buttock of the creature sold,
And the buyer leans over and snips
His mark on one of the animal's hips.

Each beast, when driven in,
Looks round at the ring of bidders there
With a much-amazed reproachful stare,
As at unnatural kin,
For bringing him to a sinister scene
So strange, unhomelike, hungry, mean;
His fate the while suspended between
A butcher, to kill out of hand,
And a farmer, to keep on the land;
One can fancy a tear runs down his face
When the butcher wins, and he's driven from the
place.

Snow in the Suburbs

Every branch big with it,
Bent every twig with it;
Every fork like a white web-foot;
Every street and pavement mute:
Some flakes have lost their way, and grope back
upward, when
Meeting those meandering down they turn and
descend again.
The palings are glued together like a wall,
And there is no waft of wind with the fleecy
fall.

A sparrow enters the tree,
Whereon immediately
A snow-lump thrice his own slight size
Descends on him and showers his head and
eyes,
And overturns him,
And near inurns him,
And lights on a nether twig, when its
brush
Starts off a volley of other lodging lumps with a
rush.

The steps are a blanched slope,
Up which, with feeble hope,
A black cat comes, wide-eyed and thin;
And we take him in.

Suspense

A clamminess hangs over all like a clout,
The fields are a water-colour washed out,
The sky at its rim leaves a chink of light,
Like the lid of a pot that will not close tight.

She is away by the groaning sea,
Strained at the heart, and waiting for me:
Between us our foe from a hid retreat
Is watching, to wither us if we meet . . .

But it matters little, however we fare –
Whether we meet, or I get not there;
The sky will look the same thereupon,
And the wind and the sea go groaning on.

Afterwards

When the Present has latched its postern behind
    my tremulous stay,
    And the May month flaps its glad green leaves
        like wings,
Delicate-filmed as new-spun silk, will the neigh-
    bours say,
    'He was a man who used to notice such things'?

If it be in the dusk when, like an eyelid's soundless
    blink,
    The dewfall-hawk comes crossing the shades to
        alight
Upon the wind-warped upland thorn, a gazer may
    think,
    'To him this must have been a familiar sight.'

If I pass during some nocturnal blackness, mothy
    and warm,
    When the hedgehog travels furtively over the
        lawn,
One may say, 'He strove that such innocent
    creatures should come to no harm,
    But he could do little for them; and now he is
        gone.'

If, when hearing that I have been stilled at last,
    they stand at the door,
    Watching the full-starred heavens that winter
        sees,
Will this thought rise on those who will meet my
    face no more,
    'He was one who had an eye for such mysteries'?

And will any say when my bell of quittance is heard
    in the gloom,
    And a crossing breeze cuts a pause in its
        outrollings,
Till they rise again, as they were a new bell's boom,
    'He hears it not now, but used to notice such
        things'?

Squire Hooper

Hooper was ninety. One September dawn
    He sent a messenger
For his physician, who asked thereupon
    What ailed the sufferer
Which he might circumvent, and promptly bid
    begone.

'Doctor, I summoned you,' the squire replied –
    'Pooh-pooh me though you may – .
To ask what's happened to me – burst inside,
    It seems – not much, I'd say –
But awkward with a house-full here for a shoot
    to-day.'

And he described the symptoms. With bent
    head
    The listener looked grave.
'H'm . . . *You're a dead man in six hours*,' he said –
    'I speak out, since you are brave –
And best 'tis you should know, that last things may
    be sped.'

'Right,' said the squire. 'And now comes – what
    to do?
    One thing: on no account
Must I now spoil the sport I've asked them to –
    My guests are paramount –
They must scour scrub and stubble; and big bags
    bring as due.'

He downed to breakfast, and bespoke his guests: –
    'I find I have to go
An unexpected journey, and it rests
    With you, my friends, to show
The shoot can go off gaily, whether I'm there or
    no.'

Thus blandly spoke he; and to the fields they
    went,
    And Hooper up the stair.
They had a glorious day; and stiff and spent
    Returned as dusk drew near. –
'Gentlemen,' said the doctor, 'he's not back as
    meant,

To his deep regret!' – So they took leave, each
    guest
    Observing: 'I dare say
Business detains him in the town: 'tis best
    We should no longer stay
Just now. We'll come again anon;' and they went
    their way.

Meeting two men in the obscurity
    Shouldering a box a thin
Cloth-covering wrapt, one sportsman cried:
    'Damn me,
    I thought them carrying in,
At first, a coffin; till I knew it could not be.'

NOTES ON THE PICTURES

p.6 *Thomas Hardy* by Augustus John (1879–1961). Reproduced by permission of the Syndics of the Fitzwilliam Museum, Cambridge.

p.15 *Boer War*, 1900, by John Byam Liston Shaw (1872–1919). Reproduced by courtesy of Birmingham Museum and Art Gallery. Photo: Bridgeman Art Library, London.

p.18 *Gift House Brethren* by William Banks Fortescue (fl. 1880–1901) Private Collection. Photo: Fine Art Photographs, London.

p.23 *Rustic Courtship* by William Henry Midwood (fl. 1867–71). Private Collection. Photo: Bridgeman Art Library, London.

p.27 *The South Downs* (detail), 1886, by Arthur (Gilbert) Williams (1819–95). Private Collection. Photo: Fine Art Photographs, London.

p.31 *Torbay* (Devon) by Sidney (J.S. Willis) Hodges (1829–1900). Private Collection. Photo: Fine Art Photographs, London.

p.34 *Sterne's Maria* by William Powell Frith (1819–1909). Private Collection. Photo: Bridgeman Art Library, London.

p.39 *The Country Dancers* (detail) by William Henry Midwood (fl. 1867–71). Private Collection. Photo: Fine Art Photographs, London.

p.43 *The Last Furrow* by Henry Herbert La Thangue (1859–1929). Reproduced by courtesy of Oldham Art Gallery, Lancashire. Photo: Bridgeman Art Library, London.

p.47 *Marsh Marigolds* by Edward Wilkins Waite (1854–1924). Private Collection. Photo: Bridgeman Art Library, London.

p.51 *Near Lizard Point, Cornwall* by Arthur Lemon (1850–1912). Private Collection. Photo: Bridgeman Art Library, London.

p.55 *The Sea-Birds' Domain*, 1902, by Peter Graham (1836–1921). Reproduced by courtesy of City of Manchester Art Galleries.

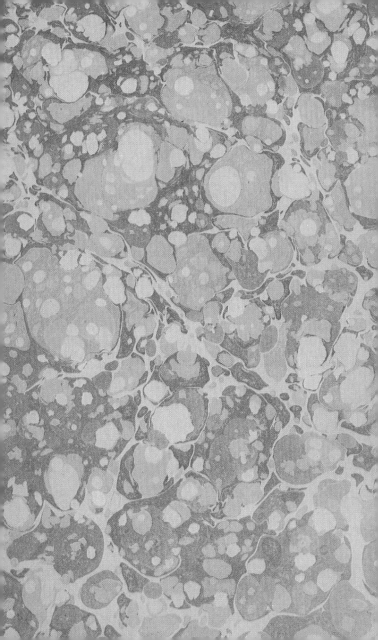